Nobody Move

poems by

SUSAN STENSON

sono nis PRESS

SONO NIS PRESS
WINLAW, BRITISH COLUMBIA

Copyright © 2010 by Susan Stenson

LIBRARY AND ARCHIVES CANADA CATALOGUING IN PUBLICATION

Stenson, Susan
    Nobody move / Susan Stenson.

Poems.
ISBN 978-1-55039-180-0
    I. Title.

PS8587.T365N62 2010   C811'.54   C2010-905256-0

Sono Nis Press most gratefully acknowledges support for our
publishing program provided by the Government of Canada through
the Book Publishing Industry Development Program (BPIDP) and
the Canada Council for the Arts, and by the Province of British
Columbia through the British Columbia Arts Council and the Book
Publishing Tax Credit, Ministry of Provincial Revenue.

Edited by Patricia Young
Copy edited by Merrie-Ellen Wilcox
Proofread by Karla Decker
Cover and interior design by Jim Brennan
Cover image: *Simple Pleasures* by Krystyna Jervis
Author photo by Josh Ward

Published by
SONO NIS PRESS
Box 160
Winlaw, BC V0G 2J0
1-800-370-5228

books@sononis.com
www.sononis.com

Printed on acid-free paper that is forest friendly
(100% post-consumer recycled paper) and has
been processed chlorine free.

Printed and bound in Canada by
Houghton Boston Printing.

The Canada Council | Le Conseil des Arts
for the Arts | du Canada

NOBODY MOVE

This book is for

Devin, Tina, James, Erika, Cole, Yvonne, Parker, Deacon, Macy and Leah.

ACKNOWLEDGEMENTS

My thanks to the editors of the literary magazines where so many of these poems were first published: *The Malahat Review, Geist, Quills, Event, The Antigonish Review, The Fieldstone Review, Prairie Fire, CV2, ARC, The Fiddlehead, The New Quarterly, The Harpweaver* and *sub-Terrain*.

"Ventricles, Aortas, Formaldehyde, Frogs" won the After Al Purdy contest, 2010. "Advice from the Heart" won the Readers' Choice Award, ARC 2008. An earlier version of "Hope Street" was commissioned for CBC's Poetry Face-Off, 2008. A portion of this manuscript was shortlisted for CBC's literary prize, 2008, and another portion in 2004. "Reader Response Theory" won *sub-Terrain*'s Lush Triumphant poetry contest, 2004. "Still Visible in the Grain" is published in *Writing the Sacred*, edited by Ray McGinnis. Other poems have been published in annual chapbooks edited by Patrick Lane and published by Leaf Press. I am grateful for Patrick's enormous generosity.

Many friends read and responded to an early version of this manuscript. Thanks especially to Wendy Morton and Amy Ainbinder. Patricia Young found the sections for the book in the tangle of poems she was handed. Patricia, thank you. Thanks also to copyeditor Merrie-Ellen Wilcox, and to proofreader Karla Decker for her keen and generous eye. Krystyna Jervis, the cover painting is perfect. I love it. Thank you. Billie Stenson, love of my life, you have the patience of a saint. xx oo

CONTENTS

What We Love About Love

Hope Street

Everyday Fools and Birds

THE ALMOST HOUR

Wonder

Not one loon,
not one flock of geese,
but birds, yes, birds,
innumerable in spring:
as light brings song,
cacophony, dawn.

NOBODY MOVE

Lovers and Lesser Men

If a man lives with two poems, / he shall be unfaithful to one

—MARK STRAND

Adding mirrors to the ceiling
is not a good idea in a master bedroom. In Vegas, you pay extra.
No one wants to see you like this.

In grade seven, Danny and Mark
used their fingers to push at the seams in your pants. You ran home.
Found a diary with a key.

Condoms are not balloons. Don't try to be funny.
Leaving a mark on a lover's neck is not *Je ne sais quoi*.
Does not say, *Wish you were here.*

Some people get along just fine
without it. Wear blue jeans, order Chinese from Jack's on the corner.
Always eat the fortune cookies first.

Looking for suggestions? Don't read Lawrence,
read Genesis (Gideon, not James), at the hotel where you will end up
alone, having followed this advice.

There's no guarantee the size of a man's hands
has anything to do with his heart. But if he cooks, sleep with him.
Garlic, gorgonzola, baba ganoush.

Ventricles, Aortas, Formaldehyde, Frogs

I couldn't grasp
the meaning of the heart

in high school. Mr. Sawatsky
and the science lab offering to help.

Clearly for understanding to arrive, he said,
be willing to take things apart.

Seize the scalpel, strip back the skin,
split wide the viscera waiting.

Not exactly the wonder of dog
asleep at my feet. *The heart leaps up.*

Four white paws crossed in dainty asides
like he's never questioned love,

rub under collar, coo.
The human heart.

Toque and gloves on the counter.
Elbows on the table. Fork full of nothing

while it swings in the air to make its point.
Done. Scoop. Swallow. The man I married.

West Coast Winter

Barefoot and dishevelled, standing outside my window
in one of the fragile cotton dresses of the poor.
She will look at me with her thin arms extended,
offering a handful of birdsong and a small cup of light
                                                    —BILLY COLLINS

Locals call them dog-eared days. So grey, the sun
keeps the head down 'til summer so you write
the final chapter of the novel and I travel to town,
teach *Romeo and Juliet*, the balcony scene, think
of our first days in love. Not young. Not Italian but
we followed the heart like school kids, endowed
with music, renaissance, rhyme, for days like this:
not a clean sock in the house, when clouds are useless,
will not rain. I believe in love: you in a meadow
barefoot and dishevelled, standing outside my window.

When I think this way, I am dreaming of hillsides
slick after a season's rain, the sea a multitude of birds
beyond Tower Point, and the forest too—flicker,
bushtit, crow, junco, a mess of sky, cedars,
oaks, fir—a trail; nothing but branches
from our road over the bridge to shore.
Is it a dream? A man and woman in love?
Light candles. Set plates, admit
we are beggars at love's door
in one of the fragile cotton dresses of the poor.

The distance between a first and second draft.
Some way to make sense of the thing, add a flood,
a war, a child. Edit with instinct not fact. Choose
one side of the bed. A heart. The body so brave
in love—knows what's to be done. What
we have touched and what we intended
when we rose from the bed, chose the same work
clothes, blew goodbye kisses on the stairs and ran,
the youngest at the door, her mind suspended,
she will look at me with her thin arms extended.

It is easy to drive the car fast. Five gears and four lanes
of highway blasted out of rock which clings high
on both sides where blue flowers roost on the rare,
flat surfaces, birthing soil out of air. A home stuck
beside the SUVs, the transports, and me. I hold
the wheel in one hand, and then two, step on it.
The car confused, signals, slows, exits at water's edge.
Something about the Gorge at noon, so much shore
caught between tides, the air exposed, contrite,
offering a handful of birdsong and a small cup of light.

Still Visible in the Grain

Because there are eggs and we have another morning together,
omelettes, coffee, cream: the knife, the fork, the spoon, eat.

Because I know what you are thinking when you knead the bread,
wait for it to rise, to bake. The waffles ready. The fruit, thick.

Butter slips into each square and over the top and trickles into the slow
soft spaces. We add syrup from one of two provinces we rarely think of

except with buckwheat and flaxseed and walnuts and lemon glaze.
No longer merely shadows, welcome maples, all.

Because the table is blond oak from Denmark,
the salt marks of the North Sea still visible in the grain.

Because our kitchen has two sinks and a window above them.
Because arbutus curls in its own time toward the light.

Surprise

No silver Buick hiding behind door number two.
No homemade tapenade with three kinds of olives.
Not even Mother's shoe on its side by the door
(three days after the funeral) as if the day she died,
she had rushed the stairs sock-footed so all we had
to do was trace those frantic steps and she'd return.
No bouquet behind a back in aisle five at Safeway.
No canned laughter. No stunned applause. Nothing
to photograph. Not a thing to toss into the ring. A
simple turn from sleep to cup your body with my own,
that first minute after alarm, everything I know,
a Monday, a Tuesday, a work day, for sure, before
Dog jumps on the bed, before Train honks at the
crossing, and I calculate that in sixty seconds
the whistle will blow again at the bridge on Selwyn
where the neighbour children must cross to school
and I must leave you here to enter the world.

Husbands

What we feel most has no name
—JACK GILBERT

It isn't easy remembering your husband's name. Late, four
a.m., say, or two-thirty on a Tuesday, he is Ishmael, coffee,
black. And after the plumbing disaster—walking the basement
in those saggy hip waders—Fernando, the ugliest gondolier
you'll ever see. Or on the ladder in December—dark and
raining again—the house lighting up like pearls on Aunt
Millie's new blouse, pure Frank. Oh, Jorge, hold me, Jorge.
And in the kitchen: Mousse. Baked Alaska. Apple pie.
A drizzle of chocolate sideswipes the chin. Yesterday, the
husband scooped up a bird the cat had carted in, wrapped it
with the classifieds and carried it to the bin. Stood a while
beside the sink before closing the lid. Brian, let's call him,
Brian, a former altar boy wearing a shirt and a tie now on
his way to the bank. Soon the mortgage will be paid! And
drinking beer for breakfast after his brother's fifth wedding, he
is Hank, lazier than firing up a leaf blower in July, pretending
he's never even seen a stove, will wait for Armageddon if he
has to for eggs to arrive sunny side up on the plate. Watch
while he hand-rolls a smoke, curled tight at both ends the way
he likes them. And for the party, celebrating twenty years,
he is Jonathan. A cute snap-on tie. No formal toast. Never
smiles for the camera. And later, watering the lawn, looking at
nothing in particular, thinking of nothing in particular, he is
Karl. Karl with a K. If it's Monday, he is Garry.
It is Garry's turn to walk the dog, so he does. He does!

Mt. Prevost. Mt. Tzouhalem.

I have loved the posterity, the wit.
The missing buttons flecked
upon the sea before spelunking
into foam after ramming into sand
beside the missing socks. Have loved
the mess of you I will follow anywhere.
The ironing: bagfuls of cotton shirts,
once each fall, once, spring. The bogs
of your boyhood: red-winged blackbirds
singing the suburban marsh blues.
For herons, patience equals bliss.
Fishing with Honeybee. Grubs and lures.
Lures and grubs. Anything worth the wait.
A subordinate clause: because, if, when.
Love the rhetorical *Mmmm?* Your *pardon-me?*
The way you can defy regret.
B.C. Lions. Vancouver Canucks.

Summer '72, Love

. . . at Deep Cove, the time she skipped her first stone, watched
the look on his face and knew she'd do it again and again

. . . on Brown Street when he repeated what the priest had to say
about God, she vowed, from then on, to never sleep alone

. . . in Saint Pascal, found a bicycle and a bottle of wine, hallelujah,
she sang on the way to the shore, and the boy tried to sing back

. . . watching the heron at Blue Bridge—that cry scared her at first,
part baby, part Mama—it could be called love

. . . at Jacob's Ladder, second step from the top beside the streetlight
the kids
from St. Aidan's had smashed—I love you he said, and sat down

. . . in the headlines: Woman Gives Birth to Three-Headed Baby;
officials say she wants to keep it: hold hard to what is there

. . . on that bus from Toronto to Denver, she stepped on a spider because
Steve said killing a spider meant it would rain, but it didn't

Knowing for Certain
You Would Not Have
the Stomach for It

You write about the chickens boarding
the train from the palazzo in single file
as if they have never been in love.
Stinking of mathematics, your husband
waits for a hearse to rise from the field.
Expecting an escort to heaven?
In this country, prepare for nothing.
What you can't bury, give away.
Write of Maman sweeping squirrels
off the feeder. She has lost her house.
No luck. I am her only son. Touché.
Forgive me, Roseanne, I loved your long hair.

Performance
in the Bedroom and Wanting to Help

My husband and I make love in a room full of men.
Neighbours, tourists, friends, even pokey brother-in-law
snuggles closer: any man who can help enters the room. So
this is a circle of men. A small Greek steps closer, savours
my palm, slides his rough face down the inside of the arm.
My husband says thank you, this woman is too much. Lets
an octogenarian wet his tongue in my eye, leave spidery
drops across my cheek like tears. Tommy, from next door,
licks an ear until my husband swats him like a fly, and
Tommy just misses the dresser drawer, caught by his father,
laughing. The circle hums. I hear a faint chant, marching
boots, French legionnaires at the top of the mound guarding
the sun, its glint and thirst no longer mirage. A stranger
holds my feet. Big Bob from Duncan rubs oil from his
diner into our skin. *Mmm*, I murmur. *Mmm*, my husband
murmurs back. The men lift us high above their heads. They
have fashioned wings. Surrendered all my shoes. There are
twelve pairs of hands supporting the weight. We won't ever
look down—we've never been married before. Set us down
on a well-used blanket. Let us make love this way for years.

Exaltations

The ear's a diviner, then
—LORNA CROZIER

Little John, the hired hand, can hear a train a mile away
with one ear on the track. "I've got my dad's ears," John says.

Tumble me down through the dark is what Liz wishes he'd say.
Tumble me down through the dark—a girl's impractical heart.

Liz hears the larks, from England, singing in the field next to the barn.
A ho-hum day, after chores. Assembling nests, cups of dead grass.

Give yourself up to what wants you, she thinks: *Weeee-oooo.*
She'll fly higher than the rest: *Weeee-oooo.* She'll fly high,

higher than the larks at Mill's Landing until John notices her
singing; how anyone can stop a train with a song.

She'll fly higher than the rest, until the big lump looks up,
until the big lump of her heart leaps out and tumbles down.

Fall in Love with the Man and Then the Circus

I.

The circus set up in the lot across the street.
One elephant slept beside a bale of straw.
Tomorrow, you will ride him.
Follow the Ouija board to the letters
your mother never lets out of the house.

2.

You slept with the clown who crawled
in the tent and made you laugh.
He wore a bright wig and shiny nose.
Flopped back and forth in those bubble-top shoes.
Traced the flower's water from mouth to mouth.

People recognized you later in the town—asked,
what is it like to sleep with a clown?

3.

Have you been thinking, is this the whole story?

4.

He met you at a party in the woods. Smoked
the Exports, the weed, another long-haired
teen in jeans and sandals.
Your mother liked his teeth.
You liked the wagon, the thick black hair.

He named the car Idi.
Said what is darkness
if there are no scars.

5.

You were nothing unless he could find a reason to save you.

6.

He tamed the tiger, named the rage.
Trapped what animals he could.
He was not crazy, yet.
Still ate with two hands.

7.

The trapeze artist said she loved him, but you saw her face.
He said you are too late to be a pretty communist
or volunteer firefighter. I am pregnant, you said.

8.

You walked the ring.
Carried the baby on the thin rope
above the bed. Borrowed
a waxy umbrella, refused to fall.

Taught the boy to hold his breath.
He was not a fast learner. Cried out
when he flipped to test the weight. You
imagined a net, fat and sloppy, down there.

Out of the wind and the weather.

Reasons Before Dinner on a Monday Knowing They Will Not Make Love

The Safeway cart let loose into the creek.
The Magna Carta. The peek-a-boo.
Big and Tall Shop on Shelbourne.
Sun-dried tomatoes on the pizza, again.

Shoeless Joe Jackson.
The itsy-bitsy spider in the drain.
Taking the cat to the vet for its forty-fifth checkup.
The kitchen needing painting. Another kind of yellow.
Medium rare with the boys at the game.

Help finding the keys.
A pie to die for.
Agree with Aunt Mabel.
It's nothing but talk.

Dog Dreams

I don't put the fire on—instead, push
two cold feet under the belly
of this green gag—your dog,
a patch of weeds the colour of mud.
He stir-fries his butt on the mat, then licks
my shin like the cupboard's bare again
and something's gotta be done. A tongue
honeyed in the dusk of a veranda,
blinking sky-tossed eyes toward heaven.
I lean in and purr. The closest I can get
to being animal. Patient, scuffle my hands
past his fur into skin. Above the forehead
a crown of scrub beats down the mosquitoes;
summer's over, I'm here with your green dog.
I am told you will return soon. Light the fire.
You know I am leaving. If a dog can dream,
take me, take me there, now.

Soft Lute of August

Let me chop apart / With my bare hands / This blurred forest
—JACK SPICER

I love the tenderness in a man's rake,
        and the affordable ache in his back after,
                or chopping wood again (without saying it aloud),

to please me. Soft lute of August in his swing and
        every window in the house open to welcome
            these sweet songs.

Thank you for the blessed axes, so many tools
        I will never understand, descendants
            of caves, lads down the lane.

A train of arbutus hugs the path
        while the garden, painfully green,
            hunkers down.

First by spring *(You with the stars in your eyes)*
        and then by summer—Come away with me.
        Come away.

Serenades over lemonade on the veranda
        on blinkered days with beans for brains.
        Lay me down.

My man's a minstrel this morning—hear him
        humming in his cabana, though he will deny
            these songs, this singing.

Last Sunday

She sometimes thinks about the convent.
A nun's life, soup slapping small bowls,
the smell of onions in the house of God.
The convent's the biggest house in town,
squat on the crest of Walton, directly
across from Our Lady of Mercy,
where Father Pearly's voice slows
at the end of his sentences like he
knows the real story and next time
will make sure we confess it: one lion
in the Flavian Amphitheatre
representing the entire world,
the universe, more likely, and one slave,
commemorating the sweet sins of the girl
who lives next door—bowling with Sam
last Sunday, a brief hand on the sleeve,
demonstrating how to twist the wrist
just so—God, the last thing on her mind and
Sam's hands, later in the Mustang, one on the wheel,
the other on her knee, a curve to hit the two pin,
—*Mary Mother of God*, it works—*by Holy*.

Amor Vincit Omnia

When I am here, I rarely leave the field.
Believe in a daisy's amatory oracles.

I can't go on, I lie. Lied.
Say, said, I let it take me.

The heart—*love me, love me not*—
offering its fingers to the dogs.

Or roosters. Any sweetie playing
with his keys between rounds.

Moths pace the caskets of before.
An old shoelace in the teeth for pain.

WHAT WE LOVE ABOUT LOVE

What We Love About Love

What we love about love are the feet.

Poor dusty things without their slippers.
Cold first thing. Forgetful later.
What is your name again?
Pentecostal in their wailing,
little toe stubs in the murk.
If the nails aren't cut, ouch.
Shoeless metatarsals. Sweet
cushions, humble in their load.

What we love about love: the eyes.

Sweet Carolinas! Squirrelly
pompoms all night long.
Everybody's grandmother
living in Vegas now.

The last train, night-capped.
Improvised parodies in blue.
Tickled pink and kootchie-koo.

What we love about love is the heart.

When everything we've ever thought
stops, bounces off the boards and scores.
The local time is 11:39.
One yip followed by a longish howl.
As plain as the nose on your face.
Believe it or not on a sunny, sunny day
in June, Elaine thought she was Elaine.

Please read the return policy.
Certain merchandise is excluded.

Not so *de rigueur*. Not so New York–
Macho–Harlem. Not so Romanesque.

What we love about love: the sex.

And whipping cream.
Believe us, we've tried everything.

Psst. The night of his conception,
she was counting origami birds.
Could have been a very different century.

We don't all have to pretend.
Right? Nine hundred and ninety-nine.

What we'll say is . . .

If a man has two poems, let him
keep them. There are martinis
and there are Chevrolets: How
many times do we have to explain?

My turtledove. My twinkle-dee.

What we love about love: its New Year's Eve.

Come here and say that!

There's something wrong with this town.
Its rococo adds up too fast.

And the runner-up is?
No kidding?

Let not the marriage of two . . .
How does it go again?

Take it outside.

What we love about love—its humongous dogs.

Luck be a lady tonight. Shagged.
Shaggier. Shaggiest. Remember, you don't have to
love the dogs because they will love themselves.

The heart is forever exhausted and hairy.

A dog needs a bath and good long shake
before it humps the vacuum again.

What we love about love—its vows.

Take out insurance, but don't
expect good luck this year.

Forgot your password again?
Copy ASTER here.

Take two of anything and call someone
in the morning.

What we love about love, its settings.

New Westminster, 1984, a pine.
Booze, Alberta, Lucky Llama Farm.
Success, Saskatchewan, Vern, she thinks.
Lonely Lake, Manitoba. Wawa, Ontario.

What we love about love: its vérité.

Shakespeare. Marlowe. Keats. Lawrence.
Its freaks and snobs. Its Fred and Wilma.
Its hampers and hangovers.
Its provoke.

Its Chekhov
early in the morning.

Its surreal *Origine.*
Fog, we think.

Its narratives.
Its plein-air.
Its cirque.
Its funk.

Its *voulez-vous?*

What we love about love—when it's fast asleep.

The mumbling of cat's paw
and parrot's flower. Silkweed.

Bloodroot or blue poppy.
Lady's slipper. Lady's slipper.

Wallflowers.
Water lilies.

No Michaelmas daisies.
No shooting stars.

Simple mourning widow.
Simple sweet william.

What we love about love—its Monday Nights.

Fond of the fumble.
Fond of the gloat.

Fond of the touchdown.
Fond of the snag.

Fond of the rushing.
Fond of the pads.

Fond of the signal.
Fond of the pass.

Fond of the hustle.
Fond of the hut.

Fond of the end zone.
Fond of the sack.

What we love about love, love.

We are willing to say we loved Everlasting. We loved Milkweed.
We loved Monkshood and Mandrake and Doll's-Eyes and Buttercup.

We loved Jessamine.
We loved Lambkill.

Lupine and Cocklebur and Fiddleneck. We loved Hellebore.
We loved Ragwort. We loved Moonseed and Gill-over-the-Ground.

Sage and Rhubarb.
Rhubarb and Sage.

What we love about love: its housing complex.

The dishes dried, the stains bleached,
the jeans ironed, the socks scrubbed,
the lawn cut, the yard raked, the kids washed,
the mortgage paid, the pension
running late for its job at the plant.
On a Saturday, love finds Lombardo
on the radio. Drinks a Coke.
Doesn't want its bed, so waltzes,
easy now, a *one-two-three:*
the partner, the living room;
Granny too old to dance, keeps time,
the spoons on one knee.

Small-Town Girl

Sex is all talk and watered-down perfume in the last stall on the left
of the public can beside Town Hall. Boys and flies. Natter and thumbs.

She knows it's out there somewhere, and all she has to do is find it.
Walk like she's not going anywhere: a small-town stride, barefoot

and bowlegged: trains and tongues on every corner, cousins, too
many to count. Church on Sundays, no matter what.

This is the body. This is the blood, they say, but not much else.
Out Shore Road, she cuts back a half mile through Old Plumber's yard,

passes the men fixing rails, slips under *hey-there* whistles. The cluck
in their tongues is the lake as it crawls a little closer: sun-drenched,

she has to find the right trail, *yoo-hoo* to the crowd of Catholic aunts,
lippy shimmer, bitch of gulls. Eyes like hawks. And feet to match.

All that summer—she breathes deep, opens her eyes—hasn't got a clue.
Knows the sun's noon-high and her life so far, a cartoon cry—*This-is-it!*

Hurricane Hazel: October '54

Is it so simple? Red lips, a dance and flask of gin?
Almost thirty, and wasn't love supposed to pull
on the heart? Dad took her fishing. *Pike. Rainbow.*
Mom had no idea—*Cutthroat*—how beautiful she was.

Hurricanes used to be named after women.
That fall was H—Hazel waltzing through town
like nobody she knew ever needed second-hand shoes.
The whole town stood by the windows to watch.

Mom said she can't believe they were driving in it, but
in those days no one let a girl stay out past ten.
It should have been a date made in heaven, a slow
drive home after the show, not this rumble and whirl.

The right parents for me, sure, but for each other?
Who knows what brings us to the altar.
Eighty people dead. And the lake looked calm
despite the whole street buried there.

They called in the army and swept the banks with sticks.
Worst storm yet. Took pictures from planes pawing the air.
Anyone who knows the past, knows the future. Tell me,
what kind of wind would have stopped them?

First Kiss

She wants to see him again. Bolts through the back door,
six steps to the gate, no creak at the hinge, nothing but air.

Mona! Wrenched back by the voice: dishes, ironing, folding,
sweeping, dusting, peeling, shining: cabinets, trophies:
    phew.

She wants to kiss him again. Under the pine tree, under
the shadow of the pine, spring feels green in the chest.

Mona! Heartbeat, natural. Her father wouldn't like him.
Dirt under nails. Hair in the eyes. No name to speak of.

She wants to kiss him again. Those lips—soft! Like a girl's!
She has to kiss him again. She just has to find him.

Proof

A woman grates a block of cheese and watches it push through
the metal in separate lines, like thin-armed women reaching
between the bars of a prison cell to touch the sleeves on the other side.
Women from the old country, her mother, maybe, wanting
the attention of the man in the brown coat, the kind of man, in this
crowd, no one notices. She can't think of her mother now.
It is late. There are children, ways of doing things, two dogs.
She polishes the table. The room is dark. Winter, maybe. Yet,
sometimes, before she lights the tapers, her own breath suspends
within the room, so it is possible the train car she's seen in movies
has no door, and a woman somehow reaches the one she longs for,
through the air, touches the sleeve, and then, the small arms
of the daughter continue to grate the cheese.

During the Non-violent Communication Workshop, I Neglect to Rescue the Fly

spotted in the soup. The fly had arrived at the exact moment
the silver ladle extended its glorious OH! from the tureen
(in the middle of the seminar), and the fly, a little bored,
it would seem, turned on its back like an honorary visitor
to the mud baths of Versailles, soaking the vernacular
through its wings—statistics, leeks, miracles, lime.
Haphazardly, those insect eyes fixed on mine (the ones
from the science text, magnified); but not in panic
as you might assume, no, no; in wonder,
as the insect sank before I had a chance to save it;
before the man in the silk suit and spectacular tie
buzzed the spoon to his mouth,
connecting the fly unquestionably
to the gloom in Monsieur's dark gullet,
the backstroke, presumably,
perpendicular now to my ravenous remorse.

HOPE STREET

Sweet Vesper Gale

We made our speech from the wind's voice
singing to earth when the moon sleeps
and in weariness after hunting
the red throat of fire the white tongues of rain
                    —AL PURDY, "IN THE BEGINNING WAS THE WORD"

We made our speech from the wind's voice:
bursts, flaws, squalls and williwaws. The rattle
of a kitchen window, tent flap, tin can out of tune.
Pamperos, Simooms, Siroccos, the Anas,
shrivelled and waned, anonymously god-fearing.
And yet we somehow knew there were others
in the offering—the chewy Venus breeze or
Prospero's tempest flying home on a whim.
Chinook. Whack. Whammy. Wreck.
We made our speech from the wind's voice

singing to earth when the moon sleeps
and we were not ashamed. It was not a time
of thinking out the darkness. Hymns,
ballads, chants, duets at the Odeon.
Do, re, mi, fa, so, la, ti, do: Jacob's Ladder,
filtered with light through the cock-eyed clouds.
We knew nothing of rhetoric, denouement.
Singing made us strong. Strength made us sing.
Impure maestros with our roulades and rap
singing to earth when the moon sleeps

and in weariness after hunting
still we couldn't stop—linguistic stalkers
with our etymologies: our earnest tongues,
our hounds, our setters: Tallyho. Tallyho.
We inched; we arched; we huddled; we humped.
We syntaxed. We collated. We crosshaired.
Crouched on the bellies of the lexicographers.
We libraried our way into bestiaries, into Bibles,
into trilogies, into texts and cookbooks, concordances
and in weariness after hunting

the red throat of fire the white tongues of rain
we made a wish, a covenant, a promise.
We named the stars, the sheepdogs, the gospels.
We named the bliss, the quagmire, the cabbage.
We named every line on a woman's face.
Betrayal. Jackrabbit. Love. Caulk boots.
The common wren. The stammer. The wail.
Lily. Kook. Stock. Muck. Marsh. Willow.
Bastard and fishing hole. Gallows. Gawain.
The red throat of fire the white tongues of rain.

Windstorm Beside You in the Blue Chair

You buy the beautiful house
but the dog never likes it.

Your children say it's boring and
your husband falls in love with golf.

Your cat runs away with a pound of butter
on its paws.

The mother-in-law tacks the petit point
of the ex-wife above the mantel.

There's a cricket in the bathroom,
and guess what song he's singing?

The milkman can't find the driveway.
You're positive it was there yesterday.

Claudia calls six times. The priest moves in.
The spiders have their babies when the guests arrive.

Granny sprains her ankle
playing bocce ball in the backyard.

The neighbours don't like you.
They bring more zucchini.

The pool table's
been missing for weeks.

Scares Me to Death

Some days I am good for nothing.
Get up at eight anyway
pull on sweater, raincoat, boots
head to the beach
where the first thing I do
is scare a heron half to death.
Which side of the cove
did you wake up on I yell
not loudly, because soon the rain
starts slap-slapping the morning
and water won't talk to you
if you get on its bad side
like Granny's finger
hitting the table
whenever she wanted
the last word. Period.
She'd rub a circle 'til
the Formica cried mercy.
Mercy, all that pushing
and rubbing got our attention.
I don't want to go outside either.
But when the roof quiets a little,
I grab my toque and gummies,
find a good dry spot under a tree.
Newcomers say it's depressing.

Reader Response Theory

the woman is running down the road
past the yellow house
and if the line above had read walking
it would be a very different poem

what if the woman was crawling down the road
past the yellow house but the house was not really yellow
because yellow is not a colour for houses in this town
so it must really be a jail with yellow bricks and grey mortar,
the colour of jails in this town and the woman is running or walking
or crawling past it so the road easily becomes
the road you were running on that day you ran past the yellow house
but had to make it look like you were really walking so nobody'd get
any funny ideas and realize you were not running down the road past
the yellow house at all but running away
from the yellow house and all that time it felt like you were crawling
not running not walking, crawling and what if
you were not a woman at all but a man running this road

the readers would need to know what kind of man you were because
men in poems are much harder to see

easy to see a woman running down the road past the yellow house
what kind of reader will question a woman running down the road
past the yellow house or assume she must have a reason for running
because the poem says she is running but the poem does not say that
she is running away from anything unlike you that time in stanza two

you were definitely running away from something so she
must be running away from it too and if the man was also
running down the road past the yellow house the reader
would want to know where the man was running to because
many readers will assume the man would be running toward
something and not away from anything but it's the woman
who is running down the road
past the yellow house and that is all you are told

Hope Township

The truth
is passed from this farm to that,
even in a drought—we believe
we have it made.
No time to feel sorry for us.

Silos, hogs, corn,
we always test the wind.
Four corners. One township.
We're farmers drawing a line.

In these parts, the rain's a secret
for twenty miles. Wild? You call it.
Deal. Rain is worth talking about
but never in mixed company.

Aunt Lorelei tells it with her bones.
Left knee aching, partly cloudy.
Soap won't suds? Good riddance.

Remember, you can't hear
the highway, somebody's dead.
Road spooked with worms?
She's not saying.

To Vivian Who Volunteered

The first time
we wove for you
it was dark wool spun
at the local market.
You visited our home
economics class,
a red cap of curls.
Skin so white, we reached
for our dolls again,
dressed and undressed
the future. Grade nine
on the hill: Port Hope.
You rarely spoke.
Silence taught us to weave.
I remember your voice rose
once, the colour of father's barn,
to catch the awkward weft,
sometimes, the smell of earth.

Home

1.

35 John Street's not far from 18 Smith Street, where years ago
the whole Catholic slew wrangled and wheezed. Don't think
it's ignorance gets you here—it's not and tell you why! 35 John
Street in 1969 is two years after Grandpa died, four years after
Granny. Your father sitting pretty in the Whitby Mental.
Finally, the family's breathing again.

2.

Any rooms but these. There's a bear behind the door. Boo.
These stairs are cold—sit because? *Three to a bed and? I'll show
you but? Cramps and elbows so?* Runny noses, pooh. Polio and
drowning. Pneumonia and grenades. Penny for your thoughts?

3.

I'll be home for . . . I'll be home . . . I'll be . . . I'll . . . I . . .

4.

Stupid. Stupid. Stupid. Stupid. Stupid. Stupid. Stupid. Stupid.
Stupid. Stupid. Stupid.
Rosemary.

5.

Touching a girl's hand to help her down from the cart—the
future—one moon over Lake Ontario, full, low, tempting you
to walk on water, follow that swath of light like some kind of
red carpet placed there just for you, for your sweet, unblinking
heart. It's not just Peter, you know, waiting for Jesus in those
god-awful waves.

6.

John Street. Centre of town, the flat bit, two blocks from the
river, the valley floor between east and west where everybody's
looking. Tracks still head north to Peterborough, but no trains
do.

But
Shoulda
Shoulda
Shoulda
Shoulda
rings loud as ever.

A slow haunt rising through an open window.
A hot plate's hum and a baby's bawl.
The slack jaw of autumn right before snow.
A clap of thunder. Come, Love, I'll carry you home.

Lullaby

She sings to her infant for the first time,
a mother's tongue, the language she hums.

Her song stretches like skin
over the body of the woman she was.

I have heard such songs. How they live
wild outside the township lines.

At the roadside shrine, a young nun
not knowing I am watching, sleeps.

Baskets collecting flowers, singing.
Not yet knowing the child is dead.

Hope Street

I wore a sheet over my head and held on
to Stephanie's hips for dear life as we made the holy
processional to Bethlehem (on our knees) down the centre of
the aisle of the little hall on Hope Street.
We were camels and Catholic. It was dark. Heat
rose from little knots everywhere inside us. Later,
at the crèche, we cradled the soft animals carved
from a brown and useless wood. How we prayed
for the cows. Believed light beamed down from heaven
to warm the world. We drew straws. Who gets the baby?
Jesus in the rocker made of clay. Plonked him down
near the window, a star crayoned with an even hand.
I stayed then until he fell asleep beside the lambs.

Confession: Saint Michael's

Miss Bar pointed at me, said,
Tall to the back where Louis,
a quarter inch shorter, hunched,

both hands in his pockets,
against a pew. Then she said,
You have to tell Father you're the last.

Too much to remember in grade one
in the big church in the big line,
waiting for a turn behind the curtain.

We'd practised for weeks,
six-year-old penitents in pinafores.
Who would forgive a forgetful child?

Bless us, Father, for we have sinned.
Sins in our best church voices. Louis
shushing any last-minute recitations.

I waited in the dark confessional
for the hidden man to slide back the grille:

These are my sins. No, wait, Father,
these are my sins and this is my last confession!

The Diviner

My grandfather had only one dream: the radio playing
in her hair, his eyes the colour of Dizzy's breath
after his last set, five encores and still
the crowd's unsatisfied, a sweaty horn, a smoky water.

My grandmother was always tired.
Twelve kids. A depression. Two wars.

I never heard her dream,
perhaps she'd given up on them by then,
but I like to believe that if she were to do it again
she would put extra cinnamon in her apple pie,
teach her seven sons to laugh
and she'd cry at Billy's funeral
despite her Protestant upbringing.

(Billy's the one who drowned in the harbour
when the maples rustled outside her bedroom window
like film through a projector in a quiet movie house,
the stars spinning their way through smoke.)

Over his skin
a white and shiny melody relaxes when she steps forward
from the wall of the barn. She smells his father's aftershave.
He has decided this one will be his wife
humming while she makes him lunch,
the radio turned up, the children gone swimming.

When he makes love, he hears a familiar song—
a slow aria of trills, a glissando of dreams,
percussive clicks drifting across her
like sluggish currents from ancient wells.

Lineage

Why I think of her this way, I'm not sure.
Is she at the station? In the café?
I don't even know her first name.
Kathleen? Francesca? Sarah? Rae?

I like to imagine her in a bath, a clawfoot tub
filled to the neck with the hottest water she can stand.
Through a veil of steam, pregnant, one leg bends
so the heel rests on the tap like in the movies,
easing the weight of the baby in her belly
as the afternoon drifts toward evening.

I have never seen a picture, only know
the pieces of the story others eagerly tell—
the colour of her hair, the tale of her lover
serving overseas and while he was gone,
she married someone else. I've heard
other stories, too. Have you?

I heard the story about my grandfather
returning from war, returning the way
some men return to the women
they have left behind, to the promises
they courted. Not young girls anymore,
women have children now, and husbands, too.

After war love waits for a man in an armchair
next to an arched window in a florid sitting room.
Love takes his hand so he lets her lead.
A place must exist. Lead on.

He reads her the way he's been taught
to read maps, the soft lip of her thigh
under the accustomed roar from air,
hair pulled back and wisped to bun.
When they land, it will fall
to the shoulders. He will weep.

Did the knock at the door surprise her?
The woman who will become my grandmother?
Mrs. Taylor? Mrs. Taylor? Was she in the kitchen,
new husband at the store?

The sun might have lit the road like it does now.
The earth must have turned to look back.

Off Air

Open the door of the fine-looking house to a musical theme,
catch a mother in pearls and sweater set and a father in a tie
and a short-sleeved shirt. Children laughing in the yard. Plastic
bat with a string. Sterile gauze in the cabinet. No blood on the sheets.
While in the real kitchen, a man fries onions, hopes his wife will
have saved enough from her cheque to grab a little ground beef at
O'Rileys, and maybe a mickey to go with it too. Already drunk,
he forgets where he is. Onions burn the pan. He was supposed to
pick up the meat and make the hash and feed the kids and get them
bathed and off to bed and scrub the pots and fold the load before she's
home at midnight but instead he sits here at the table, head slumped
in his chest. The kids curl into the armchairs, the sofa, the stairs. By
the time the wife steps in, the TV screen's got that grizzled look as
if the whole world's sleeping and what the hell is she doing awake?
Onions burn the pan and the smoky smell seeps through the plaster
into the wood. She puts her purse on the table, opens it. Flips to a
pack of Cats, takes one, lights a match. Good long drag. Catches a
glimpse of herself in the window, wisp of hair behind an ear. Flicks
the butt in the sink, scrubs.

Hell in a Handbasket:
Sunset Seniors' Lodge

I throw things. I throw things
with the intention of hitting.
Anybody can love a pink sky,
the blood of sunshine
oozing from its pores but who
can love a by-Jesus afternoon
playing crib with the geezer at the lodge?
Alzheimer's-to-boot sad air?

My grandfather
was a right holy pain in the ass
yet Marielle loved him.
The herd-of-abandoned-hills sky.
Another gold-tooth sky.

She fed him mush with a spoon.
Her prince-and-pauper sky.
My I-can't-freakin'-believe-it's-happening.
And licked the spoon after.

Piss-in-the-bottle-now sky.
Kiss-on-the-mouth. Kiss-kiss-mouth.
Good-cop-bad-cop smooch.

Throw things. Hovercraft sky.
Throw things. Kamikaze sky.
Hold me. Hold-me-back sky.

Buggy

She put me outside in all kinds of weather,
believed in fresh air. Soap and water,
my mother's great loves. Before the automatic
washer five million women lost their hair
in wringers. Mother never trusted luck. Always
washing walls, fussing cobwebs, waxing floors,
a hinge somewhere to repair. Rags on both shoulders,
she was ready for the mountains of dirt to descend.
No peace for her between bleaching and baking,
between blazers and slacks, summer and winter.
Tied my fingers with string—*these are our sins.*
What we forget to clean. Pushed the buggy
to the front step, locked the brakes, tucked
the blankets on both sides but not too tight, a baby
needs to breathe. I used to sleep for days that way.
Sometimes, she'd forget she even had a baby. The birds
landed on the buggy's bonnet. What luck, they'd cheer,
a baby! And no one thinking to shoo the cats away.

Barrett's Terrace

I.

There's a story here. The row houses
curling at the edges like cheap hems.

Mother says, handsome is as handsome does.
Don't trust the old fool.

Wipe the oilcloth yet it still feels greasy.
That old couple by the mill keeps mutts.

No one in this house drinks water.
My father studied one word per day.

2.

And later, after she died, the carnage.
Only her twin standing by the bed.

If suddenly you forget all this, mourn.
Some ceilings more than glass.

I like the feeling that no one's looking.
Who am I kidding?

The way we live: garbage day. Not yet.
The way we lived: TV guides, TV trays, TV dinners.

3.

Daddy's coming.
Somebody meet the train.

There will be scars.
One Mississippi. Two Mississippi.

Sometimes, I lie.
Follow a stranger home.

Daddy's home.
The house squeezed dry.

4.

We grew out of ourselves.
Rootless and green.

The dead always looking down.
Waiting for a ride.

Go and open the door.
I think I can.

Just off the highway, Queen Anne's lace.
Snow. A dare. Blue.

5.

Float your fanny down the Ganny.
But it's not really a race.

The trout each spring. The fish ladder.
A never-mind, this returning.

Fair enough. You betcha.
Go dog go.

The little cat feet of denouement.
Wild in the corners. One. Two. Three.

All Risk Factors Taken into Account
(Except Being Human)

Some girls whistle with no fingers. I need four
and a year of practice in the alley. Not so bad.

Two-lipped Madsen is meowing again.
It shouldn't take so long to fall in love.

Mother whistles while she works. She is tired
of the same sad stories, the ones read at bedtime.

Fights the twinge that says, *Wanna take a ride?*
Kablooey! Rat-a-tat-tat. Fool her sad fat heart.

She sees the ones I love putting on black gloves
but says nothing. Lets us ride our way into the sun.

Pomegranates

Each act in this kitchen is a part of everything
that has brought her here. Tea. Two cups.
Serve. Her mother would tuck rags in her hair.
To straighten the brown, tug the old cloth tight.
And that grandmother always rearranging things.
The means to slip into love.
Suffering in these rooms takes years to find.
The way we teach our children to put peppermint
leaves into the steaming water. Wait. A white pot.
Cut the fruit in half. Open it. Separate. Sit.
Is it enough? Of course. Of course. Eat.

November

sends us indoors to the piles of books and socks and letters that
have sat there since spring. The newspapers delight and predict.
The TV stations quibble and quiz. The fires bloat, the souvenirs
rush past. Nobody likes November. Its thirty days. Its thirty
nights. Its horns on the cattle in the squall. Hurrying under a
tempted umbrella. To shuffle off those spiders in the corners of
each room. November ain't no hustler.
No huckster's brother, either. Believe me when I tell you:
November is always November—heads down, heading to an
even darker December when light is off duty and silence on any
morning walk will not include birds. We think we can sleep
it off. Sleep through. We can't. Each night tosses something
new into the fray—the pillows punched and aired, the lovers,
loved. In November they dragged Granny Taylor kicking and
screaming into the coffin. Who knows where she is now?
Her green straw hat?

Manet's *Olympia*, 1863

What to do with the body?
Undress it, place it on a sofa, paint
the face like the tired prostitute it is,
add a cap, high heels, bracelet, choker.
Pardon me, I forgot the black cat
in a startled pose: a naked woman,
the cat thinks, not knowing the difference
between naked and nude—the human,
excuse me, Parisian, fanatic aesthete.
The servant woman, like the cat,
looks on, fetches flowers for the nude.
Female nudes evoke pleasure, *non*?
How to enjoy the body when she's staring
at us like that. Barbaric slave Edouard!
It's like walking on the Champs Élysées, and
suddenly my wife strips off her clothes.
Art? *Non*. A woman breastfeeding? *Non*.
Pleasure? *Non*. A woman's arms, legs
exposed in the Orthodox quarter?
The face exposed in Tehran?
See what you started? *Fou!*

Aubade for the Valley

My husband started writing poetry
when his car ran out of gas on the valley road.
And for a second (the time it takes to bang a steering wheel
with both hands), regretted it. (Not being a man to act out in anger)
and only his mother proud he works at the pulp mill, and not the sawmill.
Proud he can build a fence, and is comfortable, to a point, in a lumberyard.
Proud she'd raised him practical: feed and care for the calf, keep
half the money after the slaughter. Up at dawn, squeeze the cows
with *easy-now* fingers. Learned to earn his way through the dark.

When the car ran out of gas, he snapped open the glovebox.
Why he looked there, he's not too sure, but he did. Flipped
open the owner's manual and found two blank pages,
somewhere to begin. After that, he kept writing, but hid
the poems in the basement of the two-bedroom bungalow
in Crofton, not because his first wife might find them,
but not wanting to explain them either, and knowing
if she did find them, she'd expect roses, and roses,
at any time of year, were more than a poet could afford.

Forget the Old Country

Pity, O Lord, the Hungarians / Who are tossed by waves of danger
— FERENC KÖLCSEY, TRANSLATED BY LASZLO KOROSSY,
FROM THE HUNGARIAN NATIONAL ANTHEM

George never learns to write *the good English*. His hands can
lift and cut and tie and fill the trucks. That says enough.

He learns this country in the forest, a choker, mostly, work
as thick and green as the sea, but he fights the urge to die there,

to give his boots away, and simply stop breathing. These Island
clouds suckle the sun, scold any longing for light.

He hires a housekeeper who soon becomes his wife; knows
what George needs—a farm. Takes a job at the shop to help

buy a piece of their own. Says, forget the old country;
this is Canada; we have a boy to raise and fix that stoop.

George has never been a church man. All he knows of religion
breaks the fields at dawn, prayers and chickens roosting

where they will, in the kitchen, the living room, the queen-
sized bed. *Pity, O Lord*, the eggs. George can't rebuild

an engine or wire a barn, his fences awkward, squat
foreigners always needing mending. They do the job a week

at a time as if all repairs are guided by fortune, European fact.
Calls all jobs *temporary*, because at any time he might find

himself in the middle of the sea, again, alone with nothing
but memory, the butt of his brother's plan. George Szabolcsi,

the eldest, woke in the dark Atlantic, knowing the trick:
there was only one farm and the youngest had no claim.

Some days, a Saturday, after chores, a few draft downtown,
wife at the bakery, the boy at the show, George forgets

the old country, the brother, the dark sea, heads out
the Lake Road, pats the milk cow tied to the railing.

Feast

Wasn't little Babaji grand,
walking naked into the living room

where we sat by the window
having been invited in for tea

His penis faithful, hard as a pencil
sensitive to the calm in your voice

as you read the poem aloud. The word
butterfly delighting him and you repeating

butterfly
butterfly

until the tutor scoffed,
Babaji, get dressed, pulled

at the curtains and the sash
to block the light

so you scooped Babaji into your arms
without apology

butterfly
butterfly

And left the room together,
laughing and tickling straight into the sun

Said poems are birthed
in the feast of the body

Left milk in the small tins
for strays on the doorsteps

EVERYDAY FOOLS AND BIRDS

Loss

We lose the crosswords.
We lose the *How are you?*
We lose the bacon fried first thing each Sunday.
We lose the frying pan, the lid. Eggs over easy.
We lose the funnies. *The Evening Guide.*
We lose the words: morphine, bugger, Legion.
We lose the *Heaven help you.* The *You'll see . . .*
We lose the *Drop by any time.*
We lose the doctors—Kildare, Welby, Casey.
We lose the songs, barefoot boys, cross-eyed girls.
We lose the *You made your bed. You lie in it.*
We lose the *Wheel of Fortune.* Vanna, Pat, Mom.
We lose her number. We lose her keys.

Devotion

In the yard, while my husband waters the beans
by hand, a hummingbird showers in the spray
as if the bird made the decision to visit now.
Flies to branch, shakes off excess, returns.

The same way his mother practised dying. For months,
early morning, middle of the night, he climbed her stairs.
Dark-lit, paused to put out the pipe. Thought
of what he owed and how he'd made it last.

A lip of water rises from his hand,
one bird, this small song:
how she hovers.

Moon

I made popsicles from a pineapple we'd picked
off the plant in their yard; it was the first time
they'd asked about home—small tongues taking
the ice slow. They understood I was a stranger.
Imagined *Canada* but mostly loved the vowels,
vacuous, aloof. We'd found a spring halfway to town.
Thrust our hands into the watery ground like we could
dig our way home, hunt for the valleys of snow.
I was a stranger. It's true—alpaca in the churchyard
licked our fingers clean, tried to soothe a child.
That night, my first Peruvian moon. I lifted Juan,
the smallest one, above my head to the marvel
of a planet so big, we could run our fingers round
the edges, steal its stillness. *La nieve,* he said. *Snow,*
I said. His hands now almost as cold as my own.

Sorrow

Two Afghani women mourn their brother, Ishmad.
Quick the seagulls squish the island white.

His neighbours call him mad. He said,
I wish they would take me as I am.

Quick the seagulls squish the island white
as saints take off their clothes.

I wish they would take me as I am,
an evangelist, quiet, among the poor,

as saints take off his clothes,
painting the everyday fools and birds,

evangelists, quiet among the poor,
make it this far. Hush now, it's only rain

painting the everyday fools and birds,
poaching the fields with sunflowers.

To make it this far, hush now, it's only rain,
wet with those long yellow tongues,

poaching the fields with sunflowers,
while the neighbours call him mad,

wet with those long yellow tongues,
two Afghani women mourn their brother, Ishmad.

Infidelity

It has nothing to do with luck or skill.
It is not a Roman wheel or flood,
nor streetlight's drift into a room.
It is Margery standing still
in her tight dress. The one
you loved. Alone and
nobody looking, rub
your eyes. Dog
barks. Can't
go back to
sleep.

Leaving

The day she dies—a string of pearls
on her bedside table, ham sandwich, white

bread, stories of Guy de M. turned down.
And the ambulance arriving, a red light

but no siren swirling through the room
—brothel now? Mother, small in her small

nightgown, Kleenex in the left hand, whisper
of whiskey in the glass, slap of lipstick on the rim.

Prayer

The first time
she makes love
bats weave the sky
like wild kites
in the hands of boys
tempting power lines
and please stand back.

A quick nod to St. Agnes
and fingers crossed
as pants fall to the knees
when sex has no sheets
no time to undress.

But if he proposes and
she accepts, tonight's
etched in stone, a story
to share over wine.
But he does not propose.

She keeps no blanket.
No gentleman's coat.
The moon rises slow.
If there is blood, let it
return to the earth.

Mirror

She knows her dreams
are the pick-up-your-feet type.
No black bears in this backyard.
She knows when you look at her
you do not dream of caviar or
Siberian waiters serving only you.
She knows her small world: the black
bear she chased out of the bins
beside the house is actually a story
someone told her, a story they said
she could keep. She knows
where you hide the vodka.
That later she'll take the glass
from your tired hand, rinse it,
wipe the rim twice, set it down
to drain 'til morning; she knows
you won't remember the bear
in the bedroom, why, when she
wakes you, the mirror is cracked.

Certainty

And so the watcher throws himself into l'envers
— DON MCKAY

Pish, pish, pish and the bird should come
but the dog barks thinking *pish* a new command,
positive you're saying *fetch* or *biscuit. Good boy.*

Pish, pish, pish and a bird's all wings.

You must note
the long-short shriek, grip
the five-buzzed click.

You tried
the *who, who, who.*
Even tried the cage,
but still there's a breast,
a tail, a pattern on the beak.

Sugar, sugar, honey, honey.
Pish.

You're on two legs and your lips
pish. Trick the bird into this wish,
two simple seconds of flight or is it
leaf tremble? Shift of branch this time
or is it feather? *Give in. Give up.*

And the dog, frantic now, can't help
himself, barks, jumps, attacks the air
before you're sure of what you've seen.
Good boy. And the dog, too.

Qualms

Tell yourself what matters.
It probably is time to sit
in the chairs you dragged
three blocks from Rosie's
garage sale to the back
to the front to the back
of the garden. Tell yourself
it's not the end of the world.
Falling and landing here.

Fear

It smells like a woman in a room choosing a hat.
Gussied and slow, the baby laughs.

Fog smacks the bees awake; the woman
prays for more. Chooses white, felt, perfect

for a visit to the sanctuary, but not today, not yet.
The baby sleeps. He is blind, will not waste one dream.

Like the osprey looping the homely moon
towards shore into all it knows:

A sky that breaks first, loses.
Any sky that breaks, loses.

Awe

Everybody's leaving.
I can hear the crows' convention
at the funerals, the farmers latched
to sticks in the fields. How far back?
How far back to find merely awe?

These days only Henry feeds the sparrows
from his tongue. What I don't understand,
why he put his ladder against the sky
and started climbing. Forgive me, I am old.
Only the big grudges remain.

A day stretched out from end to end must thin
and what seemed once the most important thing
falls eventually, soundless, exact: the same light
upon the dead calf,
upon the pillow.

If I have to choose, I choose
the nights the crows convened
near the trees but never landed.

Faith

She has not yet swept the deck or confessed her grief over the sad, sad
state of the silverware, the garden, Paul. She has not yet begun to
apologize. She waves from inside the shop. She approves. She
reviews. She beelines. A baby must be baptized / a husband
dusted / a mistress forgiven. She arranges flowers for the dead by
scent not season. She tests pies, scrubs sinks, irons shorts. She never
rests willingly. She does not notice the deer loping across the meadow
the mornings it is time to slough off summer and most of fall. She
never remarks on the shadow of the fox in her headlights on the way
home, so she never thinks how beautiful it is. She will not catch the
hare changing colour after the first snow. She can't say exactly how
the first layer of ice spreads its thin sinews across the pond that has
been on this property so long, she has never questioned what could
have come before—her mother, maybe, picnicking with that first love,
wild berries, elder, blue—believing war was over, that this grass, this
blanket, this basket, would always mean she'd have something to
claim.

Praise

We
waited
to cut
the cord

would
not
rush
his
first
breath.

The body
shy in that
hospital
room.

We
took
him
home
to sleep
with us.

A night to believe in the world:

that
bed

big
enough

for
its own

small
moon.

Notes

The line *Lovers and Lesser Men* is from Irving Layton.

"Mt. Prevost. Mt. Tzouhalem." is for Billie Stenson.

Give yourself up to what wants you is a line from Marlene Cookshaw.

"The Diviner" is for Grandpa and Grandma Hills.

"The Feast" is for Gwendolyn MacEwan.

How far back to find merely awe is a line from Sharon Butala.

The almost hour is a line from Charles Wright.

"Praise" is for Cole.

JOSH WARD

SUSAN STENSON's work has been published in many Canadian literary magazines, most recently *The Malahat Review*, *The New Quarterly*, *Event*, *Prairie Fire* and *The Antigonish Review*. She has received numerous awards for her work, including the Rona Murray Prize for Literature, *Monday Magazine's* people's choice award for Best Book of Poetry, and the Hawthorne Poetry Award, as well as awards in the *Arc* Poem of the Year Contest, *subTerrain's* Lush Triumphant contest, *This Magazine's* Great Literary Hunt, and the League of Canadian Poets National Poetry contest. Susan's poetry has been featured on buses as part of the Poetry in Transit program and in various locations during the National Random Acts of Poetry Week. Susan calls Victoria home, and when she isn't writing poetry, she teaches English and creative writing to high school students in the Saanich School District and co-publishes *The Claremont Review* (selected as Magazine of the Year by *Write Magazine*). Her publications include *Threshold: Six Women, Six Poets* (Sono Nis, 1998), *Could Love a Man* (Sono Nis, 2001), and *My Mother Agrees with the Dead* (Wolsak and Wynn, 2007).